Goal Setting For the Equestrian

- A Personal Workbook -

KATHY FARROKHZAD

Copyright © 2016 by K. Farrokhzad

First Edition – January 2016

ISBN

978-0-9936696-6-8 (Paperback)

978-0-9936696-7-5 (eBook)

All rights reserved.

No part of this publication may be reproduced in any form, or by any means, electronic, or mechanical, including photocopying, recording, or any information browsing. Storage or retrieval system, without permission from the publisher.

Cover Photograph by Natalie Banaszak

Published by:

Full Circle Equestrian

P.O. Box 216,

Ballinafad, ON, Canada N0B 1H0

www.horselistening.com

Contents

How to Use This Book 7

1. What Does Rider Improvement Really Mean? 10

2: How to Decide On Your Riding Goals 14

3. Skill Development Plan 19

4: Annual Overview 34

5. Monthly Overviews 37

6. Special Events 103

Now Go! 116

Samples 117

*"A dream written down with a date becomes a goal.
A goal broken down into steps becomes a plan.
A plan backed by action makes
your dreams come true."
- Greg S. Reid*

GOAL SETTING FOR THE EQUESTRIAN
A Personal Workbook

HORSE LISTENING

How to Use This Book

This is not an ordinary equestrian book.

It was borne from the need to have a structured, organized, but individualized goal-setting guide for the equestrian rider and/or trainer. We frequently discuss the value of setting riding goals but there are not many books that help you put your thoughts down on paper where you can see them, evaluate them, re-visit them and let them help you make progress over the long term. This workbook is a long-term reflection and documentation of your progress and experiences with your horse.

Your goals can be anything related to horses. You might want to do ground work. You might want to think of riding goals. Maybe you're interested in teaching your horse some tricks.

You might also be interested in setting goals for yourself. These can be skill specific (using your inside leg to outside rein) or they might be physical (breathe every second stride at the canter). You might have emotional goals (stay calm and release your lower back when your horse tenses up) or maybe you want to work on specific patterns (be completely familiar with Level 1, Test 1).

Maybe you can think of other types of goals as they relate to horses.

The purpose of this book is not to tell you what goals you would like to aspire to. In fact, as you work through the book, you might choose to change the format. There is no one telling you that you *have* to stick to the ten goals that are included in Chapter 6 (although I think that is a good starting place and fairly possible to be successful at).

However, the structure is planned deliberately for horse and riding goals. The information presented at the beginning is there to help you formulate your own goals. It gives you some understanding of where to start and how to be purposeful with each step. The idea is to guide but not dictate.

GOAL SETTING FOR THE EQUESTRIAN
A Personal Workbook

HORSE LISTENING

You are encouraged to use this book throughout the year (or whatever time frame you set). Even though you will begin with a set of specific goals in mind, chances are that your plans will change as time goes by. You might not meet the goals, or your horse might need additional practice for certain skills. In any case, come back to this book regularly to re-evaluate where you are at particular times.

Using this book, you start the planning process with defining your specific overarching goals. These are the goals you want to accomplish within a year's time frame. These are your "dream" goals – there will ne many smaller steps required to reach these goals.

Next, you will take a look at the whole calendar year and plug in the goals. When will you be working on them? In any case, the yearly calendar will give you an idea of how you predict the timeline will work.

Add in any special events as they arise. These will likely be points in time throughout the year when you will be accomplishing something more than just your daily training: a competition, a riding trip, a performance, a schooling date at your friend's farm.

The monthly calendars are to be used to break down your annual plans into smaller time frame. Here, you can slot in your rides, lessons, and ground work – anything you do day-to-day. You can decide what you want to do a month ahead, or a week ahead, or even come to the calendar after the fact to document what you did.

The weekly reflection sheets give you space to document your thoughts. You can evaluate how things went and what you'd like to do next!

Come back to your goals once a week and document your results. This way, you can look ahead but also look back to evaluate what changes need to be made for the future. Hopefully, you will document all your initial goals, but then write over, scratch out, mark up, and write notes in the margins. Make this a working document of your riding journey over the year (or season) and let it help you pave out a path for your riding progress.

One note to keep in mind about goal-setting when horses are involved: *you might need to change your goals time and again, reflecting your and your horse's needs.* The

GOAL SETTING FOR THE EQUESTRIAN
A Personal Workbook

horses will always tell you how you're doing. Listen carefully and you'll get plenty of information from your equine friend, and/or from your instructor.

Don't be too concerned if you thought you could do something only to discover that your horse wasn't nearly prepared enough for it. Instead, think of how you can take a few steps back to develop the basics before moving on to more advanced skills.

This is an excellent book for the horse owner, rider, riding instructor, horse trainer, and riding student. You can apply this format to any aspect of horses - so take a few moments to read Chapters 1, 2 and 3, then write in what you'd like to see happen for you and your horse over the course of the next year, or months.

Good luck, and happy Horse Listening!

GOAL SETTING FOR THE EQUESTRIAN
A Personal Workbook

HORSE LISTENING

1. What Does Rider Improvement Really Mean?

* Please note: this theory can be adapted for every horse-related skill development including ground work, trick training, all riding disciplines and driving. We will discuss riding skills here but feel free to insert your preferred method of learning with the horse.

In horse riding, the concept of improvement is quite different than other goals we set in life. The key to progress rests in the fact that there is a rider and a horse that both need to develop as a *common unit*. In other words, a rider's level of improvement is tied into the horse's and vice versa. There is no way around it. Both are dependent on each other and cannot be separated.

The Rider Factor

Horses rely significantly on the rider's skill level. This can be easily proven when you let someone else ride your horse. Let's use the canter as an example. We'll assume that you have a pretty good understanding of the canter aids, and you and your horse canter on and achieve nice shoulder-ins at will. But the new rider is only just learning to canter, and suddenly, your horse (that always canters right off your seat) is scrambling, falling to the forehand and trotting off. You'll notice quickly that your horse will respond differently to the new person, because his ability to perform his skills are tied into the rider's coordination and use of aids.

Another example: let's say you get a chance to ride the horse of your dreams. One that is highly educated and "dances off into the sunset" with his international level rider. Chances are, even if you are fairly strong on your own horse, you end up not being quite as fluid on the super-educated horse, perhaps because your aids or timing are not refined enough for what the horse is used to, or because you have a tighter "feel" to your aids.

The level of education of the rider makes a significant impact on the horse's ability to perform.

GOAL SETTING FOR THE EQUESTRIAN
A Personal Workbook

The Horse Factor

The horse also plays a role in the rider's development. What he knows and can do impacts a rider's daily experience.

A rider's learning curve can also be dependent on a horse's ability. This is the point behind the old adage: "Green horse and green rider don't mix." Since the uneducated horse doesn't know the aids, and is in the most significant learning stage of his life, he will benefit from a rider that already knows how and why to apply aids so she can help him develop *his* skills.

This fact is easily proven by playing a fun game of "musical horses". Switch horses with a friend and see what happens. If you normally ride a horse that has difficulties with canter, and then get on one that has "canter" as his middle name, you'll understand very clearly how you as the rider are tied into that horse's abilities. You will likely be able to canter along all day, and even do new things in the canter (like try a shoulder-in for example), simply because the horse has an easy time getting into and maintaining the canter. That is his special skill.

Improvement of a Team

No matter how you slice it and dice it, you're a team with your horse. Your abilities are dependent on each other.

There is one other puzzling (but inspiring) fact to equestrian improvement, that can once again be easily proven if you watch a horse and rider develop on their journey together. Any time you notice a rider improve her skills, you will discover that the horse will also improve. Since the horse is limited to what the rider can do, the horse suddenly resolves maybe even long-term problems when the rider overcomes a challenge. This fact is also demonstrated when a more advanced rider (trainer) can get your horse to do things you've never even dreamed of.

GOAL SETTING FOR THE EQUESTRIAN
A Personal Workbook

HORSE LISTENING

Goal setting fact for riders: in order to improve your horse, improve yourself - keeping in mind what your horse needs.

There is no way around it: you must improve in order for your horse to improve. You just need to figure out what your horse needs, learn that skill, and be able to *consistently apply* it so that your horse understands what he should do.

It's an Investment

Everything you learn on one horse can be transferred to other horses. Whatever skills you develop, based on your horse's abilities and needs, *will be with you as long as you ride horses*. You will be better able to influence *other* horses thanks to what you learned from your horse.

On the other hand, other horses will teach you new things that you might not have learned on your horse. For example, your easily cantering horse probably never made you break down your aids to know *exactly* how you teach canter to a horse that has difficulty with the transition. So with a new horse, you might have to realize that you need to straighten the horse, half-halt so that he doesn't fall to his forehand, ask him to strengthen from behind, and calmly and consistently ask for the canter transition.

Some people say that the key to becoming a good rider is to ride hundreds of horses. As each horse provides new challenges, your skill set improves. You can also apply what you've already learned to new horses and "listen" to learn from their responses.

GOAL SETTING FOR THE EQUESTRIAN
A Personal Workbook

But most of us don't all have hundreds of horses to ride! Many of us don't even have access to more than a handful of horses, at best, if we ride in a riding school.

So the main question that needs to be asked is: what do you need to learn to be able to improve your horse's skills? What do *you* need to change, keeping in mind your horse's needs, to improve your skills as a combined unit?

When Things Don't Go Right

Many of us equestrians are in it because of our love for the horse. We are intrinsically motivated and self-disciplined. Sometimes we might even be overachievers, quick to offer help and quick to look at ourselves when something goes wrong.

It is those same qualities that might make us frustrated or upset when things don't work out. What happens if we don't meet our goals? Will we be so driven that nothing matters other than the achievement of the few thoughts we have in this workbook? Or will it cause us to give up on our riding goals altogether?

I hope not. That love for the horse will keep bringing us back for more.

All skill acquisition has a "plateau" phase when nothing seems to change. There is also a phase when things get worse before they get better. It happens to both ourselves and our horses, and these situations are a natural part of any kind of learning.

The purpose of this book is not to put extra pressure on you to work towards "perfection" (whatever that means). In fact, it's quite the opposite. Within these pages are opportunities for reflection, evaluation and spaces designed specifically for changing goals to meet your specific needs.

If things don't go the way you expect them to, use these pages to reflect, repurpose and redirect your energy. Then go the next day and do something different.

GOAL SETTING FOR THE EQUESTRIAN
A Personal Workbook

HORSE LISTENING

2: How to Decide On Your Riding Goals

We all have dreams for our horses and ourselves. It is always good to imagine what we will be able to do in the future, and dreams are integral to giving us motivation to go through the more difficult, skill-acquisition phases of riding. When you're having a hard time getting a simple lead change, for example, and you keep getting the outside lead time and again despite your inside aids, you might tend to lose sight of why you even want to bother.

This is when your dream will keep you inspired, interested and willing to keep trying. Your dream will bring you back the next time, keeping you on track even if your immediate goals haven't yet been achieved.

The problem is that having dreams isn't enough. We can all imagine ourselves riding in complete harmony with our horse, but there is a lot to accomplish before that vision can become reality.

This is when having well-defined, specific goals is essential. What are you going to *do* to achieve your dreams? If you listen to Yoda, you'll know that the only way to reach your dreams (and goals) is to do.

Just do. Then listen (to your horse).

Feedback

After you do something, you'll get feedback. Often it will be your horse "telling" you to change something in your plan. Other times, it will be your own body figuring out coordination, timing, or feel that indicates that something does or doesn't feel right.

If you listen carefully enough, you'll also recognize the "yes" answers your horse gives you. There is nothing nicer than trying something new and having a soft-eared,

GOAL SETTING FOR THE EQUESTRIAN
A Personal Workbook

looser (through the body), bouncier horse in response. Then you know you're really on the right track!

Of course, the most common form of feedback you can get is from someone on the ground. It can be your instructor (highly recommended), a clinician, a judge or a friend with a good eye and knowledge.

These days, you can also get someone to video your ride and then you can watch it while you're still on the horse's back, or in the comfort of you home after the ride. In any case, outside feedback is essential and irreplaceable in helping you to achieve your riding goals.

Setting Realistic Goals

In horse riding, there are several things to consider in order to set yourself up for success. The first thing to keep in mind is that the goals have to be realistic - for both you *and* your horse. It might seem obvious, but not everyone truly understands the interconnection between the rider and horse, in terms of goal setting. You should consider your horse's ability as well as your own.

For example, my horse is working at the beginning of second level (dressage) but isn't confirmed in all the movements. In considering my goals with him, I know that I have to ride to his level even though I've ridden to higher levels myself.

On the other hand, if I could ride another horse who is already working at third level, I could easily go into the second level show ring within a month. The horse would be ready and my skills would be more than adequate for that level. The combination of our abilities would allow us to set completely different goals than with the first horse.

It works the other way as well.

When I was a first level rider, I had the opportunity to ride a fourth level horse. That was amazing for me because I could learn so much from him, in a much shorter time frame. However, just because the horse could ride at that higher level didn't mean that I

GOAL SETTING FOR THE EQUESTRIAN
A Personal Workbook

was miraculously "perfect" at the higher level. Setting goals for myself on that horse would mean that I had to consider my limitations and work on those. Of course, I could achieve my rider goals significantly sooner if the horse were already educated to know what to do when given specific aids.

Below are five factors and corresponding examples that go into how you can set reasonable and realistic goals. If you can meet each factor with your intended goal, then you will be on your way to actually achieving the results you are aiming for.

1. Motivation - Why?

The first thing to identify is why you are interested in pursuing a new skill.

Knowing the "why" of the movements or skills you learn is essential not only because it informs the "how" of the skill, but also because you will be able to make informed decisions that help you set yourself and your horse up for success.

2. Identify the basic skills required to complete the new skill.

Let's say you want to start working on shoulder-in. Every time you attempt it, your horse breaks into a walk and/or steps to the inside of the ring, off the rail.

In order to accurately prepare your horse for the shoulder-in, you would consider the more basic skills that are required to help you and your horse be more successful. For example, you would need to have an easily forward-moving horse. Without forward, you won't get the lateral. Then you'll need a horse that understands a basic inside leg aid. Then you'll be sure to establish a soft but effective outside contact that will help guide your horse's bend and direction.

You get the idea. Before you start something new, make sure you understand all the sub-skills that are required. Ensure that your horse is mostly confident with the basics before you move him onto more challenging movements. When (not "if") he falters, you will know exactly what you can go back to so that you can reestablish a more basic, but more correct, movement.

GOAL SETTING FOR THE EQUESTRIAN
A Personal Workbook

Always be willing to break things down to the basics before moving on. Come back to the basics time and again just to refresh you and your horse.

3. Set goals for other aspects of riding.

We want to develop more than just the physical skills. Mental and emotional aspects develop the confidence of riders and horses. Riders need a complete enough knowledge base to know what to do when something happens. Then there is the attitude factor that develops over time - a good attitude makes everything easier and takes the rider a long way, while a less desirable attitude will always limit the rider and block the horse from performing at his best.

Make sure to consider and include any of those areas in your goal setting work, so that you may be aware of all the factors surrounding your learning.

4. Detailed descriptions of your goals.

The more specific you can be, the more you will have in the back of your mind while you ride. Rather than saying you want to work on "suppleness" for example, you can break that concept down into several specific movements and "feels" that will result in suppleness: riding forward, feeling throughness, using half-halts, developing roundness in the horse, shifting the horse's weight back to the haunches, lightness in the contact, etc. Break down each goal into several smaller, more achievable goals and improve those to meet your overarching expectations.

5. How will you measure goal attainment?

In horse riding, the achievement of your goal will have to be measured differently than, say, finishing a project or making a sale at the end of your presentation. Goals are more flowing, more open-ended when it comes to horses.

Of course, skill acquisition will be the end result of your goal setting, but mastering a skill may take months, sometimes years to fully develop. As you already know, mastery is a lifelong journey in riding. However, you might also know that without a doubt, if you

GOAL SETTING FOR THE EQUESTRIAN
A Personal Workbook

practice with support, guidance and dedication, skills will become easier and your horse will improve right along with you.

Measure goal attainment by recognizing when movements are becoming easier. Even if they are not perfect, notice the incremental improvements of both you and your horse.

6. Find the balance between too many goals (not achievable) and too few (not challenging enough).

Let's say you set a goal to clear two-foot jumps with your young horse, but you are concerned that he'll stop or turn away at the last minute. Your own lack of confidence might contribute to his reluctance, especially if he is young or inexperienced. When you decide on your goals, start with something you know you are confident enough to ride through. Then increase the level of difficulty incrementally. Maybe you can start with low jumps or cavalettis, to help develop the confidence you both need.

There it is! Identify why you're setting your riding goals. Know your basics and always come back to them while you and your horse are learning new skills. Be sure to address all the aspects of riding including mental and emotional growth and requirements. Detail all the simpler skills that are required to achieve the new skill, and use those as needed to develop confidence. Practice frequently and recognize the various steps to mastery. Keep in mind that you don't want to overwhelm yourself or your horse with too many goals at once.

GOAL SETTING FOR THE EQUESTRIAN
A Personal Workbook

3. Skill Development Plan

In this section, you're going to work out the 10 general, overarching goals you would like to reach this year. These are the grand goals, the ones that are going to combine several sub-skills to achieve.

Examples:

- CrispTransitions
- Smooth Changes of Direction
- Invisible Spooks (that's a personal goal of mine)
- Calm, Confident Rider
- Accurate Timing of Aids

However, you're going to work on making the goals much more specific using the S.M.A.R.T. method outlined on each page. This method will help you to truly clarify your thoughts and set precise, measureable goals that you can identify clearly during your ride.

Setting S.M.A.R.T. Riding Goals

S.M.A.R.T. goals have been applied to all areas of life - from business to personal development. There is value in adapting the S.M.A.R.T. methodology to horse riding and training. In this chapter, you will set your main goals for the year. There are only 10 overarching goals - that should be plenty over the time frame of a year. Feel free to add more or change your initial goals in time.

Each goal has a S.M.A.R.T. breakdown that is designed to help you decide on the clearest, most tangible goal you can. Go through the series and then decide on your goal.

Before you begin, here is some background information to clarify the meaning of each part of the acronym. I've related each section to horses and riding.

GOAL SETTING FOR THE EQUESTRIAN
A Personal Workbook

This S.M.A.R.T. system was originally published in: *Doran, George T.* **"There's a S.M.A.R.T. way to write management's goals and objectives.**" *Management Review 70.11 (**Nov. 1981**): 35. Business Source Corporate.<u>EBSCO</u> . 15 Oct. 2008.*

Specific

Pinpoint the exact goal you want to achieve with your horse. For example, "flying changes on a straight line" might seem fairly specific. However, you can go a little further and be clearer in your mind: "Flying changes on a straight line between K and M, starting on the right rein, changing to the left rein, maintaining an uphill balance, with a steady tempo."

The clearer you can be on your desired outcome, the more specific you can be with your aids and intention.

In riding, black & white is much better than gray, for both you and your horse.

Measurable

How will you know if you've achieved your goal? In our case, we are looking for small moments of progression toward our ultimate goal. For the flying change example, we could say that we have achieved our goal when we can get one clean change over one length or diagonal of the arena. (This goal would be suitable for a third level horse and rider.) More advanced goals could require two or more changes over the same amount of space.

GOAL SETTING FOR THE EQUESTRIAN
A Personal Workbook

Attainable

Is your goal reasonable and realistic? Well, if you want this particular goal to be attainable, then you should be fairly adept at the prerequisite skills that go into completing correct flying changes. You should be able to do straight, balanced simple changes (canter-walk-canter). You should have a good handle on both shoulder-in and haunches-in. You should be able to get your horse to "sit down" for two or three strides in the canter. You should also be able to get a surge of energy (impulsion) at will within the canter. The horse should be evenly balanced on both reins and very responsive to leg aids.

Although these skills are prerequisites, don't be surprised if your horse isn't able to do a flying change when you first start. It might take time to develop the coordination of aids on your part to get the result you want.

Relevant

In terms of riding, "relevant" refers to how prepared you and your horse are to complete that goal. Trying to get a level 1 horse to do a flying change could be seen as "irrelevant", for example. In other words, your horse would not be ready physically or mentally to go through the exercise with even some chance at success.

The same can be true of the rider. If the rider is only just learning about leg aids and is struggling to coordinate all her aids to do a leg yield to the rail, she may have too much difficulty managing a flying change. Building up you and your horse's skills in a step-by-step manner will always give you both a better chance for succeeding at your goals.

Time-Bound

This is a key factor in the S.M.A.R.T. goals. In many situations, putting a deadline helps us stay focused and determined to complete all the tasks required in a timely manner. Not setting time limits will leave room for dawdling, not sticking to the plan, and ultimately, doing the same thing over and over.

GOAL SETTING FOR THE EQUESTRIAN
A Personal Workbook

You can adapt this concept to the time during your ride as well. For example, you can put a limit to the number of strides per gait – and do the "10/5 Challenge", where you stay in canter for ten strides and trot for five.

Alternately, you can use a reference point to determine a time limit. In the arena, you can decide to canter by the time you leave the far corner. On the trail, you can decide to canter after the next turn on the path. Giving yourself exact moments of transitions such as these helps you become more precise and clear in your aids.

Pick reasonable time frames - say, six months to a year. Set deadlines with "get out of your own backyard" events such as clinics, performances or shows. Get out there and see how you are doing when put to the test. It doesn't have to be a show, but it has to be something that gets you preparing, putting everything together and putting it all out there on a given day. Then see what your results were and work from there when you get back home.

That's it for the S.M.A.R.T. method, but I have two other suggestions for you while you set your goals. These come from both my riding and teaching backgrounds.

Write the goal last.

Start with the S.M.A.R.T. section, the bottom sections of the page and only then, formulate your final overarching goal. Make it as specific as you possibly can.

Use positive wording.

Negative words only help you focus on the negative. Instead of writing down, "don't let the horse spook to the inside of the ring," write something like, "use inside aids and keep horse looking to the inside before we approach the spooky corner." Write what you want to do, not what you don't want to happen.

Weekly Review

Take time every week or so to go over your original goals. Without a doubt, things will change as you go through the exercises. You might find your horse is much further

GOAL SETTING FOR THE EQUESTRIAN
A Personal Workbook

along than you anticipated, or had an easy time catching on to the lesson. Alternately, achieving a goal might take a whole lot longer than you thought. There could be many factors involved, some of which you didn't predict when you set the goals.

Mental/Emotional Skills:

I've added the mental/emotional factors to the goal setting exercise because in my experience, these areas are often neglected or unrecognized. While you are thinking up your goal, consider these skills as well.

GOAL SETTING FOR THE EQUESTRIAN
A Personal Workbook

HORSE LISTENING

Goal #1:

_____

Specific: Pinpoint the exact movement

Measureable: Number of attempts per ride

Attainable: How do you know you're ready?

Relevant: Why are you doing this movement?

Time-Bound: When?

Pre-requisite Physical Skills Needed:

Mental/Emotional Skills Needed:

GOAL SETTING FOR THE EQUESTRIAN
A Personal Workbook

HORSE LISTENING

Goal #2:

_____

Specific: Pinpoint the exact movement

Measureable: Number of attempts per ride

Attainable: How do you know you're ready?

Relevant: Why are you doing this movement?

Time-Bound: When?

Prerequisite Physical Skills Needed:

Mental/Emotional Skills Needed:

GOAL SETTING FOR THE EQUESTRIAN
A Personal Workbook

HORSE LISTENING

Goal #3:

_____

Specific: Pinpoint the exact movement

Measureable: Number of attempts per ride

Attainable: How do you know you're ready?

Relevant: Why are you doing this movement?

Time-Bound: When?

Prerequisite Physical Skills Needed:

Mental/Emotional Skills Needed:

GOAL SETTING FOR THE EQUESTRIAN
A Personal Workbook

HORSE LISTENING

Goal #4:

_____

Specific: Pinpoint the exact movement

[ ]

Measureable: Number of attempts per ride

[ ]

Attainable: How do you know you're ready?

[ ]

Relevant: Why are you doing this movement?

[ ]

Time-Bound: When?

[ ]

Prerequisite Physical Skills Needed:

Mental/Emotional Skills Needed:

GOAL SETTING FOR THE EQUESTRIAN
A Personal Workbook

HORSE LISTENING

Goal #5:

_____

Specific: Pinpoint the exact movement

```
[                                          ]
```

Measureable: Number of attempts per ride

```
[                                          ]
```

Attainable: How do you know you're ready?

```
[                                          ]
```

Relevant: Why are you doing this movement?

```
[                                          ]
```

Time-Bound: When?

```
[                                          ]
```

Prerequisite Physical Skills Needed:

Mental/Emotional Skills Needed:

GOAL SETTING FOR THE EQUESTRIAN
A Personal Workbook

HORSE LISTENING

Goal #6:

_____

Specific: Pinpoint the exact movement

Measureable: Number of attempts per ride

Attainable: How do you know you're ready?

Relevant: Why are you doing this movement?

Time-Bound: When?

Prerequisite Physical Skills Needed:

Mental/Emotional Skills Needed:

GOAL SETTING FOR THE EQUESTRIAN
A Personal Workbook

HORSE LISTENING

Goal #7:

_____

Specific: Pinpoint the exact movement

Measureable: Number of attempts per ride

Attainable: How do you know you're ready?

Relevant: Why are you doing this movement?

Time-Bound: When?

Prerequisite Physical Skills Needed:

Mental/Emotional Skills Needed:

GOAL SETTING FOR THE EQUESTRIAN
A Personal Workbook

HORSE LISTENING

Goal #8:

_____

Specific: Pinpoint the exact mov6ment

Measureable: Number of attempts per ride

Attainable: How do you know you're ready?

Relevant: Why are you doing this movement?

Time-Bound: When?

Prerequisite Physical Skills Needed:

Mental/Emotional Skills Needed:

GOAL SETTING FOR THE EQUESTRIAN
A Personal Workbook

HORSE LISTENING

Goal #9:

_____

Specific: Pinpoint the exact movement

Measureable: Number of attempts per ride

Attainable: How do you know you're ready?

Relevant: Why are you doing this movement?

Time-Bound: When?

Prerequisite Physical Skills Needed:

Mental/Emotional Skills Needed:

GOAL SETTING FOR THE EQUESTRIAN
A Personal Workbook

HORSE LISTENING

Goal #10:

_____

Specific: Pinpoint the exact movement

Measureable: Number of attempts per ride

Attainable: How do you know you're ready?

Relevant: Why are you doing this movement?

Time-Bound: When?

Prerequisite Physical Skills Needed:

Mental/Emotional Skills Needed:

GOAL SETTING FOR THE EQUESTRIAN
A Personal Workbook

HORSE LISTENING

4: Annual Overview

The Annual Overview is a quick visual of what your significant goals and events will be over the year. You can start the year in January, or mid-year in relation to your show season. The idea is to give you a chance to see what you want to plan, how the timing works out in relation to your other plans, and when you'd like to achieve your major goals.

Slot in your major events. Then plan out the timing of your goals. Make sure they correspond to your Skill Development Plan. In the interest of keeping it all on one page, you might need to use symbols or short forms and write them into the notes section on the next page.

Goal-Setting Challenge:

Take a few moments at the end of each week, or every other week, to re-read through your goals.

→ *Write in what has gone well and where you're at on a given date.*

→ *Write in what your next steps are at that moment, and what your next focus should be.*

→ *Use the time to reflect, establish new goals, and record your progress.*

Then get back to riding!

GOAL SETTING FOR THE EQUESTRIAN
A Personal Workbook

HORSE LISTENING

	January					
S	M	T	W	T	F	S

	February					
S	M	T	W	T	F	S

	March					
S	M	T	W	T	F	S

	April					
S	M	T	W	T	F	S

	May					
S	M	T	W	T	F	S

	June					
S	M	T	W	T	F	S

	July					
S	M	T	W	T	F	S

	August					
S	M	T	W	T	F	S

	September					
S	M	T	W	T	F	S

	October					
S	M	T	W	T	F	S

	November					
S	M	T	W	T	F	S

	December					
S	M	T	W	T	F	S

GOAL SETTING FOR THE EQUESTRIAN
A Personal Workbook

Notes:

GOAL SETTING FOR THE EQUESTRIAN
A Personal Workbook

5. Monthly Overviews

The monthly overviews give you better opportunity to plan out your lessons and rides.

Add in any special events (shows, trail rides, performances, examinations, etc.).

Add in your weekly lessons and write in your planned main focus. Also come back later and write in what you really did, and re-evaluate your next steps.

After each monthly calendar, there are 4 weekly reflection sheets. Here you can write in what you did, how things went, what feedback you received (even if it was from the horse), how that will affect things going forward, and your plans for the next week.

This is where you can become very specific. Use it like a short diary so you can come back to it in a few months to review your thoughts.

Month		Year				
Sunday	Monday	Tuesday	Wednesday	Thursday	Friday	Saturday

NOTES

Weekly Reflection

Week: _____

Rider Analysis

- Goals practiced: _____
- Goals to work on next week: _____

What went well this week? Were this week's specific goals practiced? What specific aids were helpful in achieving your goal?

What will you change next week? Consider physical and mental/emotional skills.

Weekly Reflection

Week: _____

Rider Analysis

- Goals practiced: _____
- Goals to work on next week: _____

What went well this week? Were this week's specific goals practiced? What specific aids were helpful in achieving your goal?

```
































```

What will you change next week? Consider physical and mental/emotional skills.

```








```

Weekly Reflection

Week: _____

Rider Analysis

- Goals practiced: _____
- Goals to work on next week: _____

What went well this week? Were this week's specific goals practiced? What specific aids were helpful in achieving your goal?

What will you change next week? Consider physical and mental/emotional skills.

Weekly Reflection

Week: _____

Rider Analysis

- Goals practiced: _____
- Goals to work on next week: _____

What went well this week? Were this week's specific goals practiced? What specific aids were helpful in achieving your goal?

What will you change next week? Consider physical and mental/emotional skills.

Month .... Year ....

Sunday	Monday	Tuesday	Wednesday	Thursday	Friday	Saturday

NOTES

Weekly Reflection

Week: _____

Rider Analysis

- Goals practiced: _____
- Goals to work on next week: _____

What went well this week? Were this week's specific goals practiced? What specific aids were helpful in achieving your goal?

What will you change next week? Consider physical and mental/emotional skills.

Weekly Reflection

Week: _____

Rider Analysis

- Goals practiced: _____
- Goals to work on next week: _____

What went well this week? Were this week's specific goals practiced? What specific aids were helpful in achieving your goal?

What will you change next week? Consider physical and mental/emotional skills.

Weekly Reflection

Week: _____

Rider Analysis

- Goals practiced: _____
- Goals to work on next week: _____

What went well this week? Were this week's specific goals practiced? What specific aids were helpful in achieving your goal?

What will you change next week? Consider physical and mental/emotional skills.

Weekly Reflection

Week: _____

Rider Analysis

- Goals practiced: _____
- Goals to work on next week: _____

What went well this week? Were this week's specific goals practiced? What specific aids were helpful in achieving your goal?

What will you change next week? Consider physical and mental/emotional skills.

Month				Year		
Sunday	Monday	Tuesday	Wednesday	Thursday	Friday	Saturday

NOTES

Weekly Reflection

Week: _____

Rider Analysis

- Goals practiced: _____
- Goals to work on next week: _____

What went well this week? Were this week's specific goals practiced? What specific aids were helpful in achieving your goal?

```
                                                                                
                                                                                
                                                                                
```

What will you change next week? Consider physical and mental/emotional skills.

```
                                                                                
                                                                                
```

Weekly Reflection

Week: _____

Rider Analysis

- Goals practiced: _____
- Goals to work on next week: _____

What went well this week? Were this week's specific goals practiced? What specific aids were helpful in achieving your goal?

What will you change next week? Consider physical and mental/emotional skills.

Weekly Reflection

Week: _____

Rider Analysis

- Goals practiced: _____
- Goals to work on next week: _____

What went well this week? Were this week's specific goals practiced? What specific aids were helpful in achieving your goal?

What will you change next week? Consider physical and mental/emotional skills.

Weekly Reflection

Week: _____

Rider Analysis

- Goals practiced: _____
- Goals to work on next week: _____

What went well this week? Were this week's specific goals practiced? What specific aids were helpful in achieving your goal?

What will you change next week? Consider physical and mental/emotional skills.

Month .... Year ....

Sunday	Monday	Tuesday	Wednesday	Thursday	Friday	Saturday

NOTES

Weekly Reflection

Week: _____

Rider Analysis

- Goals practiced: _____
- Goals to work on next week: _____

What went well this week? Were this week's specific goals practiced? What specific aids were helpful in achieving your goal?

What will you change next week? Consider physical and mental/emotional skills.

Weekly Reflection

Week: _____

Rider Analysis

- Goals practiced: _____
- Goals to work on next week: _____

What went well this week? Were this week's specific goals practiced? What specific aids were helpful in achieving your goal?

What will you change next week? Consider physical and mental/emotional skills.

Weekly Reflection

Week: _____

Rider Analysis

- Goals practiced: _____
- Goals to work on next week: _____

What went well this week? Were this week's specific goals practiced? What specific aids were helpful in achieving your goal?

What will you change next week? Consider physical and mental/emotional skills.

Weekly Reflection

Week: _____

Rider Analysis

- Goals practiced: _____
- Goals to work on next week: _____

What went well this week? Were this week's specific goals practiced? What specific aids were helpful in achieving your goal?

What will you change next week? Consider physical and mental/emotional skills.

Month		Year				
Sunday	Monday	Tuesday	Wednesday	Thursday	Friday	Saturday

NOTES

Weekly Reflection

Week: _____

Rider Analysis

- Goals practiced: _____
- Goals to work on next week: _____

What went well this week? Were this week's specific goals practiced? What specific aids were helpful in achieving your goal?

What will you change next week? Consider physical and mental/emotional skills.

Weekly Reflection

Week: _____

Rider Analysis

- Goals practiced: _____
- Goals to work on next week: _____

What went well this week? Were this week's specific goals practiced? What specific aids were helpful in achieving your goal?

What will you change next week? Consider physical and mental/emotional skills.

Weekly Reflection

Week: _____

Rider Analysis

- Goals practiced: _____
- Goals to work on next week: _____

What went well this week? Were this week's specific goals practiced? What specific aids were helpful in achieving your goal?

```

```

What will you change next week? Consider physical and mental/emotional skills.

```

```

Weekly Reflection

Week: _____

Rider Analysis

- Goals practiced: _____
- Goals to work on next week: _____

What went well this week? Were this week's specific goals practiced? What specific aids were helpful in achieving your goal?

What will you change next week? Consider physical and mental/emotional skills.

Month .... **Year** ....

Sunday	Monday	Tuesday	Wednesday	Thursday	Friday	Saturday

NOTES

Weekly Reflection

Week: _____

Rider Analysis

- Goals practiced: _____
- Goals to work on next week: _____

What went well this week? Were this week's specific goals practiced? What specific aids were helpful in achieving your goal?

What will you change next week? Consider physical and mental/emotional skills.

Weekly Reflection

Week: _____

Rider Analysis

- Goals practiced: _____
- Goals to work on next week: _____

What went well this week? Were this week's specific goals practiced? What specific aids were helpful in achieving your goal?

What will you change next week? Consider physical and mental/emotional skills.

Weekly Reflection

Week: _____

Rider Analysis

- Goals practiced: _____
- Goals to work on next week: _____

What went well this week? Were this week's specific goals practiced? What specific aids were helpful in achieving your goal?

What will you change next week? Consider physical and mental/emotional skills.

Weekly Reflection

Week: _____

Rider Analysis

- Goals practiced: _____
- Goals to work on next week: _____

What went well this week? Were this week's specific goals practiced? What specific aids were helpful in achieving your goal?

What will you change next week? Consider physical and mental/emotional skills.

Month .... Year ....

Sunday	Monday	Tuesday	Wednesday	Thursday	Friday	Saturday

NOTES

Weekly Reflection

Week: _____

Rider Analysis

- Goals practiced: _____
- Goals to work on next week: _____

What went well this week? Were this week's specific goals practiced? What specific aids were helpful in achieving your goal?

What will you change next week? Consider physical and mental/emotional skills.

Weekly Reflection

Week: _____

Rider Analysis

- Goals practiced: _____
- Goals to work on next week: _____

What went well this week? Were this week's specific goals practiced? What specific aids were helpful in achieving your goal?

What will you change next week? Consider physical and mental/emotional skills.

Weekly Reflection

Week: _____

Rider Analysis

- Goals practiced: _____
- Goals to work on next week: _____

What went well this week? Were this week's specific goals practiced? What specific aids were helpful in achieving your goal?

What will you change next week? Consider physical and mental/emotional skills.

Weekly Reflection

Week: _____

Rider Analysis

- Goals practiced: _____
- Goals to work on next week: _____

What went well this week? Were this week's specific goals practiced? What specific aids were helpful in achieving your goal?

What will you change next week? Consider physical and mental/emotional skills.

Month .... Year ....

Sunday	Monday	Tuesday	Wednesday	Thursday	Friday	Saturday

NOTES

Weekly Reflection

Week: _____

Rider Analysis

- Goals practiced: _____
- Goals to work on next week: _____

What went well this week? Were this week's specific goals practiced? What specific aids were helpful in achieving your goal?

What will you change next week? Consider physical and mental/emotional skills.

Weekly Reflection

Week: _____

Rider Analysis

- Goals practiced: _____
- Goals to work on next week: _____

What went well this week? Were this week's specific goals practiced? What specific aids were helpful in achieving your goal?

What will you change next week? Consider physical and mental/emotional skills.

Weekly Reflection

Week: _____

Rider Analysis

- Goals practiced: _____
- Goals to work on next week: _____

What went well this week? Were this week's specific goals practiced? What specific aids were helpful in achieving your goal?

What will you change next week? Consider physical and mental/emotional skills.

Weekly Reflection

Week: _____

Rider Analysis

- Goals practiced: _____
- Goals to work on next week: _____

What went well this week? Were this week's specific goals practiced? What specific aids were helpful in achieving your goal?

What will you change next week? Consider physical and mental/emotional skills.

Month .... **Year** ....

Sunday	Monday	Tuesday	Wednesday	Thursday	Friday	Saturday

NOTES

Weekly Reflection

Week: _____

Rider Analysis

- Goals practiced: _____
- Goals to work on next week: _____

What went well this week? Were this week's specific goals practiced? What specific aids were helpful in achieving your goal?

What will you change next week? Consider physical and mental/emotional skills.

Weekly Reflection

Week: _____

Rider Analysis

- Goals practiced: _____
- Goals to work on next week: _____

What went well this week? Were this week's specific goals practiced? What specific aids were helpful in achieving your goal?

What will you change next week? Consider physical and mental/emotional skills.

Weekly Reflection

Week: _____

Rider Analysis

- Goals practiced: _____
- Goals to work on next week: _____

What went well this week? Were this week's specific goals practiced? What specific aids were helpful in achieving your goal?

What will you change next week? Consider physical and mental/emotional skills.

Weekly Reflection

Week: _____

Rider Analysis

- Goals practiced: _____
- Goals to work on next week: _____

What went well this week? Were this week's specific goals practiced? What specific aids were helpful in achieving your goal?

What will you change next week? Consider physical and mental/emotional skills.

Month .... **Year** ....

Sunday	Monday	Tuesday	Wednesday	Thursday	Friday	Saturday

NOTES

Weekly Reflection

Week: _____

Rider Analysis

- Goals practiced: _____
- Goals to work on next week: _____

What went well this week? Were this week's specific goals practiced? What specific aids were helpful in achieving your goal?

What will you change next week? Consider physical and mental/emotional skills.

Weekly Reflection

Week: _____

Rider Analysis

- Goals practiced: _____
- Goals to work on next week: _____

What went well this week? Were this week's specific goals practiced? What specific aids were helpful in achieving your goal?

What will you change next week? Consider physical and mental/emotional skills.

Weekly Reflection

Week: _____

Rider Analysis

- Goals practiced: _____
- Goals to work on next week: _____

What went well this week? Were this week's specific goals practiced? What specific aids were helpful in achieving your goal?

What will you change next week? Consider physical and mental/emotional skills.

Weekly Reflection

Week: _____

Rider Analysis

- Goals practiced: _____
- Goals to work on next week: _____

What went well this week? Were this week's specific goals practiced? What specific aids were helpful in achieving your goal?

What will you change next week? Consider physical and mental/emotional skills.

Month .... Year ....

Sunday	Monday	Tuesday	Wednesday	Thursday	Friday	Saturday

NOTES

Weekly Reflection

Week: _____

Rider Analysis

- Goals practiced: _____
- Goals to work on next week: _____

What went well this week? Were this week's specific goals practiced? What specific aids were helpful in achieving your goal?

What will you change next week? Consider physical and mental/emotional skills.

Weekly Reflection

Week: _____

Rider Analysis

- Goals practiced: _____
- Goals to work on next week: _____

What went well this week? Were this week's specific goals practiced? What specific aids were helpful in achieving your goal?

What will you change next week? Consider physical and mental/emotional skills.

Weekly Reflection

Week: _____

Rider Analysis

- Goals practiced: _____
- Goals to work on next week: _____

What went well this week? Were this week's specific goals practiced? What specific aids were helpful in achieving your goal?

What will you change next week? Consider physical and mental/emotional skills.

Weekly Reflection

Week: _____

Rider Analysis

- Goals practiced: _____
- Goals to work on next week: _____

What went well this week? Were this week's specific goals practiced? What specific aids were helpful in achieving your goal?

```




```

What will you change next week? Consider physical and mental/emotional skills.

```




```

Month .... **Year** ....

Sunday	Monday	Tuesday	Wednesday	Thursday	Friday	Saturday

NOTES

Weekly Reflection

Week: _____

Rider Analysis

- Goals practiced: _____
- Goals to work on next week: _____

What went well this week? Were this week's specific goals practiced? What specific aids were helpful in achieving your goal?

What will you change next week? Consider physical and mental/emotional skills.

Weekly Reflection

Week: _____

Rider Analysis

- Goals practiced: _____
- Goals to work on next week: _____

What went well this week? Were this week's specific goals practiced? What specific aids were helpful in achieving your goal?

What will you change next week? Consider physical and mental/emotional skills.

Weekly Reflection

Week: _____

Rider Analysis

- Goals practiced: _____
- Goals to work on next week: _____

What went well this week? Were this week's specific goals practiced? What specific aids were helpful in achieving your goal?

What will you change next week? Consider physical and mental/emotional skills.

Weekly Reflection

Week: _____

Rider Analysis

- Goals practiced: _____
- Goals to work on next week: _____

What went well this week? Were this week's specific goals practiced? What specific aids were helpful in achieving your goal?

What will you change next week? Consider physical and mental/emotional skills.

Month .... Year ....

Sunday	Monday	Tuesday	Wednesday	Thursday	Friday	Saturday

NOTES

Weekly Reflection

Week: _____

Rider Analysis

- Goals practiced: _____
- Goals to work on next week: _____

What went well this week? Were this week's specific goals practiced? What specific aids were helpful in achieving your goal?

What will you change next week? Consider physical and mental/emotional skills.

Weekly Reflection

Week: _____

Rider Analysis

- Goals practiced: _____
- Goals to work on next week: _____

What went well this week? Were this week's specific goals practiced? What specific aids were helpful in achieving your goal?

What will you change next week? Consider physical and mental/emotional skills.

Weekly Reflection

Week: _____

Rider Analysis

- Goals practiced: _____
- Goals to work on next week: _____

What went well this week? Were this week's specific goals practiced? What specific aids were helpful in achieving your goal?

What will you change next week? Consider physical and mental/emotional skills.

Weekly Reflection

Week: _____

Rider Analysis

- Goals practiced: _____
- Goals to work on next week: _____

What went well this week? Were this week's specific goals practiced? What specific aids were helpful in achieving your goal?

What will you change next week? Consider physical and mental/emotional skills.

GOAL SETTING FOR THE EQUESTRIAN
A Personal Workbook

6. Special Events

The following pages are set aside for anything you do that is out of the ordinary. It could be a horse show, a clinic or special riding lesson, or anything that you participate in that gives you some sort of feedback. They are set up for you to outline the specific skills you practiced, the feedback and your future goals stemming from that feedback.

Use the overview section to jot down some general reminder notes of what the event was, where, what was done. Then use the rest of the sections to clarify the notes, the results and future goals.

SPECIAL EVENT NOTES

DATE

Overview

Event Name

Overall results

Clinician/Judge/Other

Original Goals

Location

Summary | Your thoughts

New Revised Goals

Skill

Skill

Skill

Skill

Skill

SPECIAL EVENT NOTES

DATE

Event Name

Clinician/Judge/Other

Location

Overview

Overall results

Original Goals

Skill

Summary

Your thoughts

New Revised Goals

Skill

Skill

Skill

Skill

SPECIAL EVENT NOTES

DATE

Event Name

Overview

Clinician/Judge/Other

Location

Overall results

Original Goals

Skill | Summary | Your thoughts

Skill

Skill

Skill

Skill

New Revised Goals

SPECIAL EVENT NOTES

DATE

Event Name

Overview

Clinician/Judge/Other

Location

Overall results

Original Goals

Skill | Summary | Your thoughts

Skill

Skill

New Revised Goals

Skill

Skill

Skill

SPECIAL EVENT NOTES

DATE

Event Name

Overview

Clinician/Judge/Other

Location

Overall results

Original Goals

Skill | Summary | Your thoughts

Skill

Skill

New Revised Goals

Skill

Skill

SPECIAL EVENT NOTES

DATE

Event Name

Clinician/Judge/Other

Location

Overview

Overall results

Original Goals

Skill

Skill

Skill

Skill

Skill

Summary

Your thoughts

New Revised Goals

SPECIAL EVENT NOTES

DATE

Event Name

Overview

Clinician/Judge/Other

Location

Overall results

Original Goals

Skill | Summary | Your thoughts

New Revised Goals

Skill

Skill

Skill

Skill

SPECIAL EVENT NOTES

DATE

Event Name

Overview

Clinician/Judge/Other

Location

Overall results

Original Goals

Summary | Your thoughts

Skill

New Revised Goals

Skill

Skill

Skill

Skill

SPECIAL EVENT NOTES

DATE

Overview

Event Name

Clinician/Judge/Other

Location

Overall results

Original Goals

Skill | Summary | Your thoughts

Skill

Skill

Skill

Skill

New Revised Goals

SPECIAL EVENT NOTES

DATE

Event Name

Overview

Clinician/Judge/Other

Location

Overall results

Original Goals

Skill

Summary

Your thoughts

New Revised Goals

Skill

Skill

Skill

Skill

SPECIAL EVENT NOTES

DATE

Event Name

Overview

Clinician/Judge/Other

Location

Overall results

Original Goals

Skill | Summary | Your thoughts

New Revised Goals

Skill

Skill

Skill

Skill

SPECIAL EVENT NOTES

DATE

Event Name

Overview

Clinician/Judge/Other

Location

Overall results

Original Goals

Skill

Summary

Your thoughts

New Revised Goals

Skill

Skill

Skill

Skill

GOAL SETTING FOR THE EQUESTRIAN
A Personal Workbook

HORSE LISTENING

Now Go!

Once you've had a chance to think through your goals and formulate them in a way that makes them achievable, there is only one thing to do: take your thoughts and ideas to the barn and practice.

Making your dreams come true likely won't happen in a linear fashion. In fact, it might be a messy, one-step-forward, two-steps back kind of progression. The fundamental joy in riding horses is the time you spend doing.

Even though you've planned your goals and put all this work into it, there is no guarantee that you will achieve exactly what you set out to do. There is the horse that has a say in the matter. Then there are your own skills that might need some polishing.

However, there is one thing that the goals will do for you. They will give you a direction to move toward. They will help you evaluate your progress and guide your efforts as needed. Finally, they will show your achievements in a clear, concrete manner. So while goal setting is an informed way of heading along on your path of horse and rider development, it's only one part.

The next step: just do. Dreams will not happen in the back of your mind. You must go to the barn. Do and then do some more. Put in the time, the days, the months. Get feedback and do some more.

Track your progress here weekly, monthly and over the year. Analyze and change whatever needs changing. Then go to the barn, and do it again.

There is no other way!

GOAL SETTING FOR THE EQUESTRIAN
A Personal Workbook

HORSE LISTENING

Samples

GOAL SETTING FOR THE EQUESTRIAN WORKBOOK
A Step-By-Step Plan

HORSE LISTENING

Goal #8:
Forward, cadenced SI with a forward seat & upper body, 5 times each way in a ride, confirmed by March 2016

Specific: Pinpoint the exact movement
Shoulder-In on the rail

Measureable: Number of attempts per ride
~~Once~~ Five times each ride, each way, the whole length of the rail

Attainable: How do you know you're ready?
Can do leg yield & bend. → time to put them together.

Relevant: Why are you doing this movement?
Helps with future lateral work & engagement of the hind end.

Time-Bound: When?
In the middle of the ride, after warm-up. Done 5 times each direction, every ride.
→ Accomplish good, forward SI by March.

Forward, cadenced shoulder-In with a forward seat & body, 5 times each way.
→ already working on it, time to polish the movement.

Prerequisite Physical Skills Needed:
Leg yield aids, bend aids. Make sure I go with the horse. Steady outside rein, ½ halts before losing balance. Inside "fluttering" rein for flexion.

Mental/Emotional Skills Needed:
- Calm: settle my mind & refocus on aids
- Persistence: to do it again even if unsuccessful
- Patience: wait for it to develop over time.
- Mental "forward": to not restrain the horse

GOAL SETTING FOR THE EQUESTRIAN WORKBOOK
A Step-By-Step Plan

HORSE LISTENING

Goal #9:

Longer legs by opening hips, straightening knees, allowing ankles to drop naturally, before/during/after every movement, to be a habit by June 2016 & not thinking about it by end of the year!

Specific: Pinpoint the exact movement

> Longer legs in movement at walk/trot/canter & in lateral movement.

Measureable: Number of attempts per ride

> Focus on it ~~during~~ before, during & after each movement.

Attainable: How do you know you're ready?

> I can do it! Just needs to become a habit.

Relevant: Why are you doing this movement?

> Better position & aids, horse can be freer.

Time-Bound: When?

> Habit to self-check by June 2016, confirmed by next year.

Need to allow my legs to be longer
→ ~~straighten the knees~~
→ open the hip
→ straighten the thighs & knees
→ let ankles drop naturally

Prerequisite Physical Skills Needed:
- strong enough core strength
- soft contact & independent hands.

Mental/Emotional Skills Needed:
Focus! Repetition & willingness to let go of the horse's sides at the right moment of the stride.

GOAL SETTING FOR THE EQUESTRIAN WORKBOOK
A Step-By-Step Plan

HORSE LISTENING

Year: 2016.

January
S	M	T	W	T	F	S

February
S	M	T	W	T	F	S

March
S	M	T	W	T	F	S
			SI			
					Clinic	

April
S	M	T	W	T	F	S
			Clinic			

May
S	M	T	W	T	F	S
			Clinic			

June
S	M	T	W	T	F	S

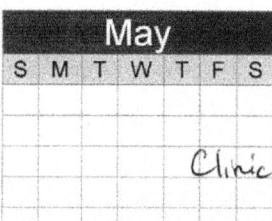
confirmed legs
Longer
Show?

July
S	M	T	W	T	F	S
			Show?			

August
S	M	T	W	T	F	S
			Show?			

September
S	M	T	W	T	F	S
			Show?			

October
S	M	T	W	T	F	S

November
S	M	T	W	T	F	S

December
S	M	T	W	T	F	S

GOAL SETTING FOR THE EQUESTRIAN WORKBOOK
A Step-By-Step Plan

HORSE LISTENING

Notes:

SI confirmed by March 2016.

Longer legs - habit by June 2016

- Weekly lessons
- Monthly clinic
- Show through the summer?

Month January Year 2016

Sunday	Monday	Tuesday	Wednesday	Thursday	Friday	Saturday
					1	2
3	4 Lesson	5	6 Ride	7	8	9
10 Clinic	11 Cancelled ~~Lesson~~	12 Ride	13	14	15	16 Ride
17	18 Lesson	19	20 Ride	21	22	23 Ride
24 / 31	25 Lesson	26	27 Ride	28	29	30 Ride

NOTES

- Lesson riding through January
- Times may change based on cold weather
- Work on Goals #8 + 9 concurrently
- Predict Cyrus' spooks earlier as he is more reactive in the cold.

Weekly Reflection

Week: Jan. 10-16

Rider Analysis

- Goals practiced: Clinic, forward. w/T, T, T/w
- Goals to work on next week: Keep working on over the back & throughness at all gaits.

What went well this week? Were this week's specific goals practiced? What specific aids were helpful in achieving your goal?

- Made it to the clinic! → see Event report.
- The basics we discussed during the clinic will be helpful in my overarching goals.

What will you change next week? Consider physical and mental/emotional skills.

- Slow down my aids, slow down my body + thoughts BUT expect a quicker/more confident response from Cyrus.
- Start adding in the SI + longer leg goals.

- More ½ halts after down transitions.
- Seat to ½ halt for a more uphill transition.
- Do more but less! Shorter/longer strides in the gait.

SPECIAL EVENT NOTES

Date: Jan. 12, 2016

Event Name: Clinic — Janet

Overview

Slow down to keep Cyrus more focused (not the riding & movements, but my thoughts & aids).

Add lots of W/T, T and T/W transitions especially in warm-up + cool-down.

Overall results: Be a more active rider!

Original Goals: Work on collection.

New Revised Goals: Go back to simpler transitions, change myself!

Skill	Summary	Your thoughts
Predict spook	Ride actively long before the spook happens!	Worked so well! Eliminated spooks.
More ½ halts after T/W trans.	I stop riding when Cyrus walks	Need to remain active + ½ halt 2, even 3 times after the down trans!
Over the back	Combined w/ half-halts	Used a tiny bit of seat (not a lot) into the walk trans. C's back rounded instantly!
Uphill trans.	Seat / ½ halt	Suddenly brought C off the forehand and light in the contact
Do more but less	Trans. within the gaits	Keep the horse busier **not** by doing a million different things, but by changing stride length in the same gait → shorter stride to longer stride — WHILE in whatever gait/movement.